~~LOT~~ on Business, Travel, and Culture in China

by

Eddie Flores, Jr.
Elisia Flores

Illustrated By

Jon J. Murakami

Copyright @ 2014 by L & L Franchise, Inc.

No part of this book may be reproduced in any form or by any electronic or mechanical means, including information storage and retrieval devices or systems, without written permission from the publisher, except that brief passages may be quoted for reviews.

All rights reserved.

ISBN-10: 0985819219
ISBN-13: 978-0-9858192-1-7
Library of Congress Control Number: 2014945794

First Printing
Illustrated by Jon J. Murakami
Designed by Brandon Dela Cruz

L & L Hawaiian Barbecue is a registered trademark of L & L Franchise, Inc.

Published by:
L & L Franchise, Inc.
931 University Avenue, Suite 202
Honolulu, Hawaii 96826
Phone: 808-951-9888
Fax: 808-951-0888
Email: info@hawaiianbarbecue.com
Website: www.hawaiianbarbecue.com
Facebook: www.facebook.com/hawaiianbarbecue
Twitter: www.twitter.com/hawaiianbarbecue
YouTube: www.youtube.com/hawaiianbarbecue

Printed in Hong Kong

Dedication

To my lovely wife, Elaine, and my two daughters, Elisia and Ellice, who had the patience and tolerance to work for me at L & L Hawaiian Barbecue. This book could not be completed without the support and encouragement from my family and the L & L Hawaiian Barbecue staff.

Acknowledgements

Thanks to my office staff for their editing and design: Elisia Flores, Ellice Flores, Elaine Flores, Brandon Dela Cruz, Josie Akana, Kelly Gan, Raymond Cheng, Caroline Guira, Andrew Lee, Kanoe Fragas, Bryan Andaya, and student intern, Rachel Oda.

Thanks to my friends who reviewed and critique my book: Henry Parwani, Manuel Flores, Richard Lim, Brenda Foster, and Gerald "Gerry" Chang.

Thanks to Jon J. Murakami for his funny illustrations. He is an artist who can capture people and scenes with humor and sensitivity.

Thanks again to my wife, Elaine, and my two daughters, Elisia and Ellice, for their patience, love and understanding, and encouragement during this arduous endeavor.

Introduction

This book reflects Eddie's funny and entertaining way of "talking story" on his sixty years of experience dealing with Chinese in the United States and in China. Eddie was born in Hong Kong and immigrated to the United States when he was sixteen. He has been very active in the Chinese community in Hawaii, and has extensive business dealings with Chinese in the United States and in China.

This book is written explicitly with China in mind. Most of the customs and traditions may be similar for Chinese in Hong Kong, Taiwan or other countries. However, there are many differences within China itself. With over 1.34 billion people, many local and regional customs and traditions may vary.

The book focused on some of the key customs and traditions in an exciting and hilarious manner. You will learn many aspects of the Chinese society, travel and business. Each section has an interesting lesson about the Chinese people, a tip on how to deal with them, a "did you know?" factoid, and finally a cartoon to emphasize the key issue. It is a very easy and amusing reading. This book is invaluable to anyone wanting to travel, to do business, or to understand China in a concise and humorous way.

Table of Contents

Introduction — 5

Chapter 1: History, Geography and Government — 8

Chapter 2: Chinese Culture and Superstitious Beliefs — 16

Chapter 3: Verbal and Non-Verbal Communication in China — 38

Chapter 4: Chinese Dining — 54

Chapter 5: Doing Business in China — 82

Chapter 6: Travel — 108

TERRIBLE FENG SHUI MASTER

Did you know? According to a Feng Shui master, you should not keep a broom in the room of a sick or dying person because the broom will sweep away the life of that person.

Chapter 1
History, Geography and Government

A Short Chronological History of China

China has a long recorded history, going back over 5,000 years, making it one of the oldest civilizations in the world. The Chinese are very proud of their culture and history. A brief time-line from the beginning of Chinese civilization to the modern era is chronicled below.

- The Peking man was the earliest human being who lived in Zhoukoudian, a village southwest of Beijing, about 400,000 to 500,000 years ago.

- The Xia dynasty (2100 B.C. – 1600 B.C.) was the first dynasty in China. China continued to be ruled by dynasties until the "Double Ten" revolution, October 10, 1911.

- The Chinese developed skills in farming, silkworm-raising, tool making, construction, and trading between 2100 B.C. to 221 B.C. During this time, Chinese civilization flourished with many thinkers and philosophers such as Confucius.

- The first emperor of the Qin Dynasty, Qin Shih Huang, unified all of the Chinese feudal states in 221 B.C.

- Between 618 and 907, Chinese civilization flourished under the Tang Dynasty by trading with countries all over the world.

- The British started the Opium War against China in 1839. The war ended with the Treaty of Nanjing in 1842, which ushered in a "century of unequal treaties." Under the treaty, the island of Hong Kong was ceded to the British in perpetuity and four "treaty ports," including Canton and Shanghai, were opened to the British.

- Sun Yat Sen successfully led a revolution to overthrow the Qing Dynasty and established the Republic of China in 1911.

- In 1949, the Chinese Communist Party drove the Nationalist government to Taiwan with Mao Zedong as the Chairman. The United States refused to recognize the Chinese Communist Party as the legitimate government of China and instead supported the Nationalist government in Taiwan.

- China adopted the "Four Modernizations" – agriculture, industry, science and technology, and national defense - set by Deng Xiaoping in 1978, welcoming foreign investments and ushering China into a new era of economic growth.

- The United States officially recognized the People's Republic of China as the legitimate government on January 1, 1979 and established a diplomatic relationship.

Tip #1 To understand the Chinese people, you have to understand Chinese history.

Did you know? The father of modern China, Sun Yat Sen, and the President of the United States, Barack Obama, attended the same school (Punahou School, formerly Oahu College) in Hawaii.

FORTUNE COOKIE SECRET MESSAGE

Did you know? Makoto Hagiwara of Golden Gate Park's Japanese Tea House in San Francisco claims to be the person who invented fortune cookies around 1890 to 1900.

A Short Lesson in Chinese Geography

China is the fourth largest country in the world after Russia, Canada and the United States. It has the largest population with 1.34 billion people. Ninety-one percent of the people are of Han Chinese ethnicity and the rest are composed of over 55 minority ethnic groups such as Tibetans, Zhuang, and Manchu.

The country has an area of 3.7 million square miles and shares borders with fourteen countries including North Korea, Afghanistan, Bhutan, Burma, India, Kazakhstan, Kyrgyzstan, Laos, Mongolia, Nepal, Pakistan, Russia, Tajikistan, and Vietnam. China has three main rivers, the Yellow River in the north, the Yangtze in central China, and the Pearl River in the south. The terrain is mostly mountains, high plateaus, and deserts in the west and plains, deltas, and hills in the east.

The climate is extremely diverse, ranging from tropical in the south to subarctic in the north. Through the years, China struggled with frequent typhoons along the southern and eastern coasts as well as floods, droughts, and earthquakes in other areas. Much of its agriculture and development are in the eastern region. There is less development in the western region of China since the land is less fertile.

Tip #2 After reading China's history, your next step is to visit the country.

Did you know? The Chinese city of Tashkurgan has about 5,000 ethnic Chinese citizens. Many of them have striking green eyes.

ACUPUNCTURE GUARANTEED TO WORK

Did you know? Acupuncture is over 5,000 years old and it is one of the oldest medical practices in the world. The original needles were made of stone, bamboo or bone.

The Chinese Government

China is one of the few countries that maintains the communist ideology. The government is authoritarian and has full control over the daily lives of its citizens. The current economic system is termed a "socialist market economy" by the West.

The Communist Party of China's power is granted in China's constitution. It controls many of the most powerful appointments, including the General Secretary of the Chinese Communist Party (CCP) and the Chairman of the Central Military Commission. Since China is a single party state, the General Secretary, as the Communist Party leader, holds power and authority over the government. Therefore, through its appointment power, the Communist Party effectively has control of the government.

The President of the People's Republic of China is largely a ceremonial title. However, typically, the President holds additional offices, including General Secretary of the Communist Party and Chairman of the Central Military Commission, making that individual the paramount leader of the country.

The electoral system is hierarchical. The local People's Congress is elected directly, and all higher levels of the People Congress up to the National People's Congress are indirectly elected by the People's Congress of the level immediately below. The political system is decentralized and the elected provincial officials have substantial autonomy in running its local matters.

Tip #3 You can impress your Chinese friends by knowing the names of the president and premier of China.

Tip #4 Always remember that the Chinese government and the Chinese people are hierarchical.

Did you know? The Chinese government relaxed the one child per family policy in 2013. China has 32 million more men than women.

BEJING HAS AN ONE DOG PER FAMILY POLICY

Did you know? A zoo in the People's Park of Luhoe in the Henan province reportedly tried to disguise a Tibetan mastiff dog as a lion.

Leave America Behind When You are in China

Be sure to leave all your notions of American laws and policies behind when you visit China. You can forget about civil rights, Americans with Disabilities Act (ADA) compliance, fair housing, federal minimum wage laws, sexual harassment laws, gun laws, free speech, and whatever else you are accustomed to in the United States. Most of these have no equivalent in China.

This does not mean that China is a lawless society. In fact, China has an enormous number of laws, and many of these laws are vigorously enforced. I recommend that you understand the Chinese laws and policies and abide by them when you are in China.

The Chinese government is very sensitive about a number of issues. You should refrain from criticism of Mao Zedong and any discussion of the Cultural Revolution, Tibet, Taiwan, Tiananmen Square uprising, Xinjiang, human rights, abortion, and Falun Gong. You do not want to alienate the Chinese government or offend your Chinese friends by raising any of these issues.

I was on a sightseeing tour with three friends in Xi'an a couple years ago. We had a great friendly and vivacious tour guide. It was a wonderful time for us all until one of my friends started a discussion on Mao Zedong's role during the Cultural Revolution. I saw the change in the tour guide's face and the rest of the trip was catastrophic. The tour guide became hostile and caustic.

Tip #5 You can make fewer enemies by staying away from issues considered sensitive by the Chinese government.

Tip #6 You can sue in a Chinese court. However, the chance of winning is probably slim. Even if you win, collection will be almost impossible.

Did you know? Chinese citizens are not permitted to possess firearms. The maximum penalty is death.

CHINESE ARE TOO INNOVATIVE

Did you know? The Chinese government has implemented a series of positive legislative and administrative actions for the purpose of improving the living conditions and social status of people who are physically or mentally disabled. However, you cannot compare American laws with Chinese legislation. They are very dissimilar and enforcement is different.

Chapter 2

Chinese Culture and Superstitious Beliefs

In the United States, we place great emphasis on personal success, creativity, and initiative. Americans value our independence and non-conformity. In China, the Chinese are taught to submit to authority and conform to the society. They are asked not to question the status quo but rather to accept it.

Chinese society is hierarchical both in business and in the family. Decisions are made at the top of the hierarchy. Mid and low level managers have little power in making decisions. The key decisions are made by the senior members, top down.

The Chinese are more comfortable knowing there is organization of authority and a hierarchical structure. The Chinese function better knowing who is superior and who is subordinate.

Tip #7 Find out who the boss really is as soon as possible and show full respect to that person.

Tip #8 Always remember that Chinese do not like confrontation.

Chinese proverb: "If you know your Chinese boss and know yourself, you can win the confidence from your Chinese boss. If you only know yourself and not your Chinese boss, you may not gain respect. If you know neither yourself nor your Chinese boss, you will endanger yourself."

THE REAL BIG BOSS

Did you know? Many Chinese employees call their employers "Big Boss" as a mark of respect for their employers and to show that their employers are at the top of the hierarchy.

What is Mianzi?

The two important words in doing business in China are Guanxi (connection) and Mianzi (face). You will see that many situations and stories are related to Guanxi and Mianzi in this book.

We will start with Mianzi. It is the most important concept that you have to learn with respect to Chinese culture. Mianzi literally means "face" in Chinese. The concept of Mianzi is deeply rooted in Chinese culture. It represents a person's reputation and prestige within the workplace, society, and among friends. The position of a Chinese person is relative to the position of their counterpart. For example, father and son, parent and child, teacher and student, employer and employee. Mianzi connotes that a certain degree of respect and behavior is expected between individuals.

When I travel to China with my Chinese staff, they know to automatically call me big boss, to walk behind me, and to open the door for me. Yet, I have never asked them to perform such menial tasks. My Chinese staff know that since I am the president of the company, I have to be treated like all the Chinese bosses in China. They do not want to lessen my position relative to my Chinese counterpart and have me "lose face."

A public insult or challenge could be a loss of face and dignity and may bring retaliation. A friend of mine, Lee, has a chain of restaurants in Los Angeles. When Lee expanded to Guangzhou, he asked his good friend, Chang, who also owned a chain of restaurants, to be a partner. During a dinner, Lee jokingly challenged Chang in front of his friends claiming that he could operate the restaurant better than Chang. Well, that was the end of their friendship. Chang lost face in front of his friends. Instead of being Lee's partner, Chang opened restaurants similar to Lee in Guangzhou to compete against him in order to save face.

A simple decline of invitation or saying no with weak pretext may trigger loss of face. For example, at dinners in China, the host quite often wants to toast and asks to bottoms up. Even though I am allergic to liquor, not participating in the "bottoms up" could potentially offend my host. Therefore, I must always apologize profusely for not accepting the liquor, but still participate in the toast by drinking tea or water.

My Chinese friends always ask what type of Mercedes I drive. I tell them that it is a SL550. Any Mercedes lower than the top model will be below my social standing. Mianzi is so important that even a poor family will buy an expensive gift for a rich relative's son or daughter's party. Chinese would rather starve than to lose face.

Tip #9 Don't ever make any Chinese lose face. They will retaliate.

Tip #10 Although you are not Chinese, you still need to understand Mianzi in China.

Chinese proverb: "People live for polished face while trees live for bark."

GOING HUNGRY IS BETTER THAN LOSING FACE

Did you know? Losing face is a loss of dignity, social standing, and honor in China. Mianzi is very important in the Chinese culture.

Guanxi is Also Very Important

Guanxi is the second most important concept that you have to learn in China. Guanxi describes the relationship that results in the exchange of favors or connections. Whenever a favor is given, it is expected that the favor will be returned in the future. In simple terms, "If you scratch my back, I'll scratch yours."

No matter who I meet in China, all of them brag about the important people that they know, such as the mayor, province chief or business person. It is important to establish and maintain relationships with influential people. With Guanxi, anything can be done.

Several years ago, my friend tried to impress me with his Guanxi. Prior to visiting him in Xiamen, he told me about the red carpet welcome I would receive. I shrugged it off as a joke and didn't think anything of it. When I arrived, I was met by several local government officials, a small band, and several young students with flowers for me. By having the right Guanxi, you will be able to facilitate your business and you will meet with fewer obstacles.

Guanxi does not have to be based on money. It could be an introduction or advice. An acceptance of Guanxi requires a return of Guanxi in another form. Many Chinese businesses are built on mutual trust. The relationship of trust takes time to develop and to nurture. Guanxi requires a harmonious relationship between the two parties in order to be maintained. Certainly with the proper Guanxi, you will be able to steer clear of many roadblocks and expedite your path to success in China.

Tip #11 To be successful in China, you need Guanxi.

Tip #12 Remember that nothing is free and you are expected to repay Guanxi.

Chinese proverb: "With Guanxi, nothing matters; without Guanxi, everything matters."

YOUR WAIT IS SHORTER WITH GUANXI

Chinese proverb: "It is not what you know, but who you know."

Confucianism

The Chinese culture is in a state of change. Many of the new beliefs in China today are counter to the traditional Confucian teaching. The younger generation's emulation of the American lifestyle and culture creates a gap between the new and traditional values. Confucianism centers on the concept of harmonious relationships. It is based on the rules and expectations of respect, loyalty, and duty between the relations of husband-wife, friend-friend, and employer-employee. It advocates honor and filial piety as well as respect for age and seniority. Such ideas remain current and are still important traits among Chinese around the world. Confucianism is an ethical and philosophical system, not a religion.

Tip #13 If you want to understand the Chinese, study the philosophy of Confucius.

Did you know? There are three million registered descendants of Confucius under his family name of Kong in China and overseas. The Confucius family has the longest recorded living pedigree in the world.

CONFUCIUS WAS RIGHT

Did you know? Confucius taught that people must be good and should respect their elders, their parents, as well as their ancestors. People should be honest, kind, obedient, polite and wise.

A Foreigner is Always a Foreigner

Unless you are born with two Chinese parents, you will always be a foreigner in the eyes of the Chinese. People may try to integrate into Chinese society, but they will always be singled out as a foreigner.

I recently read a story about a Brooklyn born lawyer named Sidney Shapiro. He moved to China in the 1940's and married a Chinese wife. Mr. Shapiro became a Chinese citizen, spoke flawless Chinese, had a distinguished career in China, and lived on the same street for decades. Mr. Shapiro considered himself a true Chinese. Yet, if you asked his Chinese neighbors, they would point to him as a foreigner.

Last year, I told one of my Chinese friends that I am writing a book on China. Although he knew that I was born and raised in Hong Kong and can read and write Chinese, his first words were "but you are not Chinese." A foreigner will always be a foreigner in the eyes of the Chinese.

Tip #14 Being a foreigner has an advantage. You are not expected to understand the intricacies of Chinese etiquette and you will be readily forgiven for any lapses.

Napoleon once said, "China is a sleeping giant. Let her sleep, for when she wakes, she will shake the world."

PRETENDING TO READ ENGLISH

Did you know? China Daily is the largest English language newspaper in China. It has a circulation of approximately 500,000. The paper is the guide to official Chinese government policy.

Chinese Superstitious Beliefs

Superstitions have passed on from generation to generation in Chinese society. The Chinese have many superstitious beliefs such as numbers, colors, zodiac animals, fortune tellers, and Feng Shui. These customs are part of Chinese daily life. There are probably very few Chinese who do not believe in some superstition. Most of my L & L Hawaiian Barbecue Chinese franchisees have to check with the fortune teller for the right date and proper Feng Shui for their grand openings. I seriously doubt that picking the right date or Feng Shui has any bearing on their success. However, I always respect their beliefs. It is important for us to understand their superstitious beliefs and show respect to the Chinese culture.

Tip #15 Respect Chinese superstitious beliefs even if you do not believe them yourself.

Did you know? Just as the number thirteen is bad luck to Westerners, so too the number four is bad luck to Chinese. In Hong Kong, a former British colony, you may find buildings with fourth and thirteen floors both missing.

FAKE MEDICINE

Did you know? Up to seventy-seven percent of the Viagra bought online may be counterfeit, and most of which are probably manufactured in China.

Chinese Zodiac Animals

The Chinese believe that every person and every animal has a role to play in society. It fits closely with the Confucian belief in a hierarchical society and maintaining harmonious relationships. The zodiac signs provide people with insights into personality as well as predictions for the future.

The zodiac animals are based on a twelve year cycle that corresponds to a different animal sign for each year. The twelve animal signs are rat, ox, tiger, rabbit, dragon, snake horse, sheep, monkey, rooster, dog, and pig.

People born in the year of different signs have distinct characteristics. For example, the rat is smart and wealthy yet timid and lacks concentration. Similar to astrology, it is believed that compatibility between different zodiac animals varies and can range from very compatible to incompatible.

Tip # 16 Have your child born in the Year of the Dragon. You will have a very popular and special child.

Did you know? There is always a baby boom in the Year of the Dragon in China. Many Chinese couples time their child's birth to land on the Year of the Dragon.

(See page 29 for Chinese Zodiac animal descriptions.)

Sheep   1919, 1931, 1943, 1955, 1967, 1979, 1991, 2003, and 2015
Sheep enjoy being alone in their thoughts. They're creative thinkers, wanderers, unorganized, high-strung and insecure, and can be anxiety-ridden. The best match for sheep is pig or rabbit.

Monkey   1920, 1932, 1944, 1956, 1968, 1980, 1992, 2004, and 2016
Monkeys thrive on having fun. They're energetic, upbeat, and good at listening but lack self-control. The best match for monkey is rat or dragon.

Rooster   1921, 1933, 1945, 1957, 1969, 1981, 1993, 2005, and 2017
Roosters are practical, resourceful, observant, analytical, straightforward, trusting, honest, perfectionist, neat and conservative. The best match for rooster is ox or snake.

Dog   1922, 1934, 1946, 1958, 1970, 1982, 1994, 2006, and 2018
Dogs are loyal, faithful, honest, distrustful, guilty of telling white lies, temperamental, and sensitive. The best match for dog is tiger and horse.

Pig   1923, 1935, 1947, 1959, 1971, 1983, 1995, 2007, and 2019
Pigs are extremely nice, good-mannered and tasteful. They're intelligent, always seeking more knowledge and exclusive. The best match for pig is rabbit or goat.

Rat   1924, 1936, 1948, 1960, 1972, 1984, 1996, 2008, and 2020
Rats are quick-witted, clever, charming, sharp and funny. They have excellent taste and are generous and loyal to others considered part of its pack. The best match for rat is dragon or monkey.

Ox   1925, 1937, 1949, 1961, 1973, 1985, 1997, 2009, and 2021
Ox is steadfast, solid, a goal-oriented leader, detail-oriented, hard-working, stubborn, serious and introverted, but can feel lonely and insecure. The best match for ox is snake or rooster.

Tiger   1926, 1938, 1950, 1962, 1974, 1986, 1998, 2010, and 2022
Tigers are authoritative, self-possessed, have strong leadership qualities, charming, ambitious, courageous and warm-hearted. The best match for tiger is horse or dog.

Rabbit   1927, 1939, 1951, 1963, 1975, 1987, 1999, and 2011
Rabbits enjoy being surrounded by family and friends. They're popular, compassionate, sincere and they like to avoid conflict. The best match for rabbit is goat or pig.

Dragon   1928, 1940, 1952, 1964, 1976, 1988, 2000, and 2012
Dragons are energetic and warm-hearted, charismatic, lucky at love and egotistic. They're natural born leaders. The best match for dragon is monkey and rat.

Snake   1929, 1941, 1953, 1965, 1977, 1989, 2001, and 2013
Snakes are seductive, gregarious, introverted, generous, charming, analytical, insecure, jealous, slightly dangerous, and intelligent. The best match for snake is rooster or ox.

Horse   1930, 1942, 1954, 1966, 1978, 1990, 2002, 2014, and 2026
Horses love to roam free. They are energetic, self-reliant, money-wise, and they enjoy traveling, love, and intimacy. The best match for horse is dog or tiger.

Did you know? President Barack Obama, Napoleon Bonaparte, Margaret Thatcher, Adolf Hitler, and Saddam Hussein were all born in the Year of the Ox.

Feng Shui

Feng Shui is a Chinese ancient art and science that was developed over 3,000 years ago. The word Feng means "wind" and Shui means "water." Feng Shui reveals how to balance the energies of a house in order to get the best health and fortune for the people living in it. It is usually practiced by Feng Shui masters who spend many years studying the ancient art. The Feng Shui master will determine the proper arrangement and architectural design to bind the universe, earth, and man together in order to assure success, fortune, or a harmonious life.

Many years ago, a Chinese investor from Hong Kong bought a hotel in Waikiki. There was a restaurant on the ground floor that was quite busy. The Feng Shui master determined that the door of the restaurant facing the street was bad Feng Shui. To correct the bad Feng Shui, the front street entrance was closed and a new entrance was built inside the hotel lobby. Instead of increasing the flow of traffic into the restaurant, it decreased. Six months later, the restaurant was closed. Feng Shui did not work for this restaurant. However, there are many successful stories and this could be just one bad Feng Shui master.

<u>Tip #17 Even though you have doubts about Feng Shui, do not disagree with your Chinese partners.</u>

Chinese proverb: To create good auspicious Feng Shui, there has to be a balance of Yin (negative) and Yang (positive) such as hot and cold or dark and light.

ANOTHER BAD FENG SHUI MASTER

Did you know? Mirrors are used to deflect or to redirect negative energy. You may see a mirror in a Chinese home or business and usually the mirrors are placed at the windows or the doors.

What are the Lucky Numbers?

Numbers are very important in Chinese culture. They can be used to select dates for a grand opening for businesses, weddings, and many other celebratory events. The actual value of the number itself is not what determines whether it is auspicious or not. Rather, it is the pronunciation of the number. If the number is pronounced in a way that sounds like a word that has a positive meaning, then that number may represent luck and fortune. Conversely, if the number is pronounced in a way that sounds like a word with a negative meaning, that number may bring bad luck.

The best number is 8. The pronunciation sounds like the word for wealth and fortune. I selected the L & L Hawaiian Barbecue telephone number to be 808-951-9888. Other numbers such as 9 could mean permanence, 2 means ease, harmony and longevity, and 6 is for continuity and success. The number could be used in combination, such as 168 which means continuance of fortune and success.

The worst number is 4 which means death or combinations such as 14 which means guarantee death or 24 which means easy death. Chinese businesses will avoid holding their grand openings on these days.

A developer was planning a high rise in Honolulu many years ago. He had a problem: The address of the project was 44. After consulting with his Chinese experts, the address was changed to 88. The condominium was very popular with Chinese buyers and the units were quickly sold out.

Even numbers are preferred over odd numbers because they bring harmony and agreement. Quite often your Chinese host at a restaurant will order an even number of dishes.

Tip #18 Remember, 8 is a good luck number and 4 is a bad luck number.

Did you know? A vanity car license plate number 18 sold for HK $16,000,000 (US $2,000,000) in 2008.

8 IS A LUCKY NUMBER

Did you know? The opening ceremony of the Beijing Olympics was 8/8/08 at 8:08 pm.

Lucky Colors

Colors are a significant part of the Chinese culture. The three lucky colors are yellow, red, and green. Each symbolizes good fortune or success and is used prominently in decoration during festivities and celebrations.

Red is considered the best and the luckiest color and it is displayed during most festivals and major events. The red color represents success, fortune, and happiness. During Chinese New Year, money is stuffed in red envelopes as a gift. Yellow is the color of royalty and the throne. Emperors were dressed in yellow and rode yellow carriages during the Ming Dynasty (1368-1644) and Qing Dynasty (1636-1911). Green symbolizes money. It brings in fortune and wealth. Quite a number of businesses, such as banks and restaurants, are painted in red and green.

Tip #19 Instead of buying a birthday card, use the red envelope and give cash to your Chinese friends and relatives.

Tip #20 Leave your white suit and white shoes at home when you go to China.

Did you know? The seventh lunar month is the Ghost month in China. The ghosts and spirits are believed to come from beneath the earth to visit the living. The Chinese ghosts are usually dressed in white.

THE COLORS OF CHINA'S NATIONAL FLAG ARE RED AND YELLOW

Did you know? The national flag of China is known as the five stars flag (wu xing hong qi). The flag is red in color with five yellow stars. The large star symbolizes the Communist Party of China while the smaller stars represent the four economic classes: workers, peasants, petty bourgeoisie, and patriotic capitalists.

Gifts to Avoid Giving

Chinese are very superstitious with the type of gift to give and to receive. A gift is always appreciated, but certain gifts could symbolize death or bad luck.

Last Christmas, I was doing a book signing for my "$266 Million Winning Lottery Recipes" cookbook at Costco. Many customers and personal friends came, and I gladly autographed books for them. However, I noticed many of my Chinese friends walked by but did not purchase my book. I finally realized that a book means "loser" in Cantonese. You certainly do not want to buy or give a "loser" gift for Christmas.

- Clocks sound like funeral ritual in Chinese. It may mean the end of life.

- Knives and scissors symbolize "to commit suicide," or "cut off relationship."

- Books mean to lose, especially to gamblers.

- Shoes is pronounced similar to break up or going a separate way. It could also mean dirt.

- Some of the other gifts to avoid are handkerchiefs, towels, umbrella, knife, gifts in four, a green hat or anything that is black or white.

Tip #21 If you want someone to pay for your wedding party, invite as many Chinese friends as possible. They usually give cash in red envelopes.

Tip #22 Please don't give books, shoes, clocks, or knives as gifts to your Chinese friends.

Did you know? The value of the gift depends on the circumstance and your relationship to the recipient. Depending on rank, the most senior person will receive the most expensive gift.

A CLOCK AND THE COLOR WHITE REPRESENT DEATH AND SORROW

Confucius once said, "The honorable and upright man keeps well away from both the slaughterhouse and kitchen. And he allows no knives on his table."

Chapter 3
Verbal and Non-verbal Communication in China

The Chinese language seems difficult for many Americans. It is complex to learn, and the characters look like a puzzle. Furthermore, there are different variations and dialects. Following are some interesting facts on Chinese language.

1. Most Chinese in the United States came from Guangzhou area. They speak Cantonese with different county dialects. However, with the influx in recent years of new Chinese immigrants from Taiwan and mainland China, Mandarin is slowly replacing Cantonese in most Chinatowns around the world.

2. Chinese seem to talk very loud. While it may sound like they are arguing, it is just part of the way they communicate. In a recent trip to Shanghai, my Chinese friend was bargaining for a souvenir near Nanjing Road. He and the seller were yelling and bickering. Five minutes later, my Chinese friend paid 50 RMB for the souvenir. Both my Chinese friend and the hawker parted ways with smiles on their faces.

3. In the United States, the surname is the last name. In China, the surname is the first name. When I first arrived in Hawaii in 1963, I met a Chinese friend with the first name Johnson. Later, I met three more Chinese friends with the first name Johnson. It was strange to find so many people with the name Johnson in Honolulu. I have not met an American with Johnson as the first name. I finally asked one of them why he used Johnson as his first name and he replied that he admired Lyndon Johnson, the 36th President of the United States. At that time, he did not realize that Johnson is actually a last name. He thought it was the first name in the Chinese language.

4. In China, the women normally keep their surname after marriage. Chinese wives may be addressed with Mrs. preceding the husbands' family name. In Hong Kong and Taiwan, the wives use the husbands' last name.

Tip #23 Have your children learn Mandarin as their second language.

Tip #24 Always address a person by their last name like Mr. Lum or Mrs. Lum.

Did you know? Li is the most common Chinese family name in China. There are over 100 million people with Li as a family name. Wang is second and Zhang is third.

AMERICAN AND CHINESE WEDDING RECEPTION

Did you know? Chinese brides have to change three times during a modern Chinese wedding reception. They start with the western dress to welcome the guests, change to a red or gold gown for the toast, and finally, a traditional Chinese Cheong Sam gown at the end of the reception.

Meeting and Greeting

Meeting and greeting the Chinese way may be more formal than what we are used to in the United States. In China, meeting face-to-face is very important. It is strongly suggested that you research the hierarchy of the organization or family of the individual prior to meeting them. The Chinese place the highest importance and give the highest respect to the most senior ranking person. It is customary to greet the most senior person first, then continue greeting everyone else based on their rank, in descending order. Do not shake everyone's hand randomly.

In America, we are used to a firm hand shake. Quite often, I felt like my hand was being crushed. In China, when you shake hand, do not use a firm grip. You should shake with a less than firm grip and slightly nod your head as a welcome gesture. Be gentle and smile as an approval of the meeting.

When you are introduced, make sure you stand up. It is common courtesy to acknowledge the introduction. If they clap to welcome you, make sure you smile and slightly bow to show appreciation. You get more respect when you understand the Chinese culture.

Tip #25 Use a light grip to shake hands with your Chinese friends.

Tip #26 Learn to speak a couple simple Chinese words or phrases to impress your Chinese friends.

Chinese proverb: "Make happy those who are near you, those who are far will come."

MEET THE CHINESE EXTENDED FAMILY OF 1.34 BILLION

Did you know? Chinese parents prefer their daughters to date boys with glasses since that may indicate the boys may have higher education and are from a wealthy family. They also prefer fair skin to dark skin.

Hugging and Kissing

Hugging and kissing in public may be universally accepted in the United States, but in China, public display of affection is not considered normal or proper. The Chinese do not express feelings the same way as Americans. Looking back at my upbringing in Hong Kong, I do not have any memory of being cuddled or kissed by my parents. This does not mean that they did not care for me. Rather, they expressed their emotions in other ways such as acts or deeds of kindness. I have many memories of my parents telling me to "take care" and of them bringing me extra food and toys.

As an American meeting a Chinese for the first time, do not greet them with a hug or kiss. Even if you have known that person for a long time, it is safer to stay away from hugging and kissing. I recall an American friend once told me that he worked in Xi'an factory for two years. His co-workers had a farewell party for him. When the party ended, he had tears in his eyes and he tried to hug some of the female co-workers to say goodbye. Many of his co-workers simply ran away from him in shock. Physical signs of affection will create an embarrassing or uncomfortable situation. A simple handshake, slight bow, and a big smile will do.

The younger generation in China, however, may display more intimate social interactions. Recently, at the Shanghai International Airport, I observed more hugging and hand holding. Not just between younger couples, but also between the younger generation and their parents and grandparents. Times have changed and the Chinese are adapting to the Western culture. However, to be safe, it is better to stay away from hugging and touching in public.

Tip #27 Stay away from hugging and kissing, especially in public.

Tip #28 To show your affection, buy a going away gift.

Chinese proverb: "You can hurt yourself more than anyone can hurt you by keeping all your feelings hidden."

THE CHINESE PARENTS ARE ALWAYS WATCHING

Did you know? China is the top developer and manufacturer of drones after the United States.

Get a Qualified Interpreter

The Chinese language is imprecise and difficult to understand. Additionally, there are so many regions in China with local dialects. The ability to communicate clearly and to interpret correctly is more complex than most people can imagine. Even Chinese may have difficulty in figuring out the correct interpretation. I attended a deposition for a lawsuit several years ago in Honolulu. We hired a licensed Chinese interpreter with a doctoral degree to translate. There were several occasions where the translator's interpretation was incorrect. Each time, I had to ask for an intermission to correct the translator. If you have a major speech or meeting, you might want to hire two interpreters and make certain that the material is properly translated before the meeting or presentation.

Jokes, jargon, and slang are especially difficult to translate. I gave a speech to prospective L & L Hawaiian Barbecue franchisees in Beijing several years ago. I used two of my funniest jokes that in America usually draw thunderous laughs. Instead of laughs, I saw grim and silent faces. I was so stunned that I almost lost track of my speech.

As a foreigner, unless you have full command of the Chinese language, I strongly recommend a qualified Chinese interpreter. In China, do not underestimate the language difficulty and barriers you will need to overcome. Although I speak fluent Cantonese, my Mandarin is only rudimentary. I am able to converse in general Mandarin but not enough to conduct business. I found that most Chinese appreciate my Mandarin, but I doubt seriously they understand me fully. Using a qualified interpreter can help you better understand the Chinese and make certain that your message is delivered properly.

When you use a Chinese interpreter, be sure to adhere to the following basic rules.

1. Meet with the interpreter and make certain he/she is qualified.
2. Have a practice session to smooth out any problems.
3. When you speak, use short sentences and pause from time to time.
4. Avoid jokes, jargon, and slang.
5. Speak slowly.
6. Talk to the host and not the interpreter.

Tip #32 Hire a Chinese interpreter who graduated from an American university.

Tip #33 Unless your Mandarin is perfect, use a qualified Chinese interpreter.

Did you know? When KFC first translated its advertising slogan of "finger licking good" into Chinese, the translation was "eat your fingers off".

BLUNDER IN COMMUNICATION

Did you know? Chinese consumers increasingly favor American made cars for their reputation of safety, luxury, and international flair. Buick is one of the most popular American luxury brands in China.

Learn Simple Chinese Words

Chinese take a lot of pride in their language. When I was attending elementary school in Hong Kong, my Chinese teacher always used me as an example to lecture the Chinese students. He said if a foreigner would take time to learn Chinese, you as a Chinese should study harder and to learn your own language.

Chinese always admire foreigners who speak the Chinese language. They are thrilled even if you say only a few words or phrases. They usually are delightfully surprised and show appreciation to the foreigner who is able to speak Chinese.

I have listed eight simple but common phrases that you can you use to "wow" your Chinese friends. The phrases are very easy to learn. For the proper pronunciation, you can consult translate.google.com or ask one of your Chinese friends to help you. If you master these eight simple phrases, you will gain respect and admiration from your Chinese friends and counterparts. You will receive a lot of "wow" from them.

1.	How are you?	*Ni Hao*	pronounced "Nee How"
2.	I am well	*Wo Hao*	pronounced "Woh How"
3.	Good	*Hao*	pronounced "How"
4.	No	*Bu*	pronounced "Boo"
5.	Yes	*Shi*	pronounced "Sher"
6.	Tasty	*Hao Chi*	pronounced "How Chur"
7.	Thank you	*Xie Xie*	pronounced "Syeh Syeh"
8.	Goodbye	*Zai Jian*	pronounced "Zay Jeahn"

Tip #29 When you meet someone, say Ni Hao.

Tip #30 When you want to show your appreciation, say Xie Xie.

Tip #31 When you say goodbye, say Zai Jian.

Chinese proverb: "Be not afraid of going slow, be afraid of standing still."

Business Card Protocol

Business cards in China are very different than those you find in the United States. I read an article about a Chinese businessman named Chen Guang Biao recently. Chen made the news when he tried to purchase the New York Times for a huge sum of money. On Chen's business card, he listed over 30 titles and positions.

For the Americans, Mr. Chen sounds like an audacious man and his titles seem incredulous. However, in China, almost every business card carries many titles to show the importance and stature of that person. It is part of the Chinese culture to list all of your positions and titles. However, do not take everything at face value. Quite often some of the titles could be nonexistent and purely exaggeration. On a whim, I once decided to investigate some of the businesses listed on my Chinese friend's business card. Turned out they did not exist!

To help you better understand the etiquette of business cards in China, I have listed a few pointers for reference.

1. When you give your business card to someone, use both hands – use your thumbs and index fingers to "pinch" the upper two corners of the business card, presenting it so that the recipient can readily read it. Similarly, when receiving a business card, use both hands.

2. When you receive a business card, it is improper to immediately put it into your wallet. Read the card with interest before you put it away. Spend time looking at the business card even if you cannot read Chinese.

3. Make sure your business cards are printed in English on one side and Chinese on the other side. It is preferable to print in simplified Chinese in China and traditional Chinese in places such as Hong Kong, Singapore, and Taiwan. When giving your business card, present it with the Chinese side showing.

4. When giving your business card, do so standing up. It shows more respect.

5. For your business cards, you may choose to list not just your title and current company, but you should also consider listing any other organization you are affiliated with.

Tip #34 Make sure your business card lists all your important titles and positions.

Tip #35 Make sure your business card has English on one side and Chinese on the opposite side.

Tip #36 Make sure you present your business card with two hands.

Did you know? Chinglish is spoken or written English that is influenced by the Chinese language. Most times it is due to improper and ridiculous English translations of Chinese.

Counting With Your Hand

If you want to impress your Chinese friends, learn the Chinese way of counting with your hands. Using just one hand, the Chinese method covers the numbers one through ten. The hand counting method may have been developed to bridge the difference in spoken language due to local dialects. The Romanized spelling and pronunciation of Chinese numbers may have been confusing when negotiating and doing business. Using hand symbols appeared to be much clearer.

I remember living in Hong Kong as a child going to the market and asking the price of items for sale. The vendor would not only say the price, but also use his hands to show me. For example, if the price was $2.00, he would have said two and also held up two fingers. Nowadays, I rarely see the hand counting method being used.

Last year, Vance Roley, Dean of the Shidler College of Business at the University of Hawaii invited a Chinese businessman to lecture on the topic of "Doing Business in China." During the presentation, he demonstrated the hand count method to the audience. To my amazement, everyone was impressed. As a matter of fact, it was the highlight of the whole presentation. Therefore, if you master the hand counting method, I promise that your Chinese counterparts will be impressed as well.

Tip #37 Learn how to count with your hand and impress a lot of Chinese people.

Did you know? Since China combined five time zones into one, the western part of China may have sunrise as late as 10 am.

COUNTING ONE TO TEN ON ONE HAND

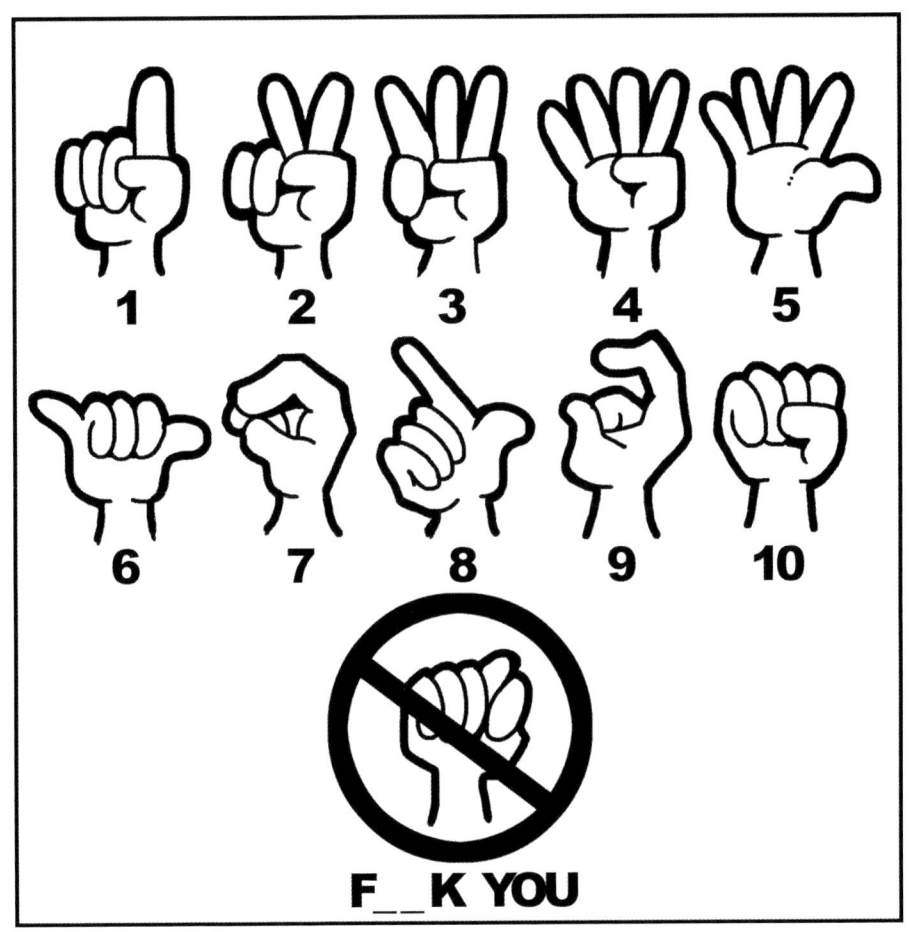

Chinese proverb: "Never underestimate stupid people in large numbers."

"Thank you for the tea" – Finger Tapping

Another sure way to impress your Chinese friends is by knowing to tap two fingers whenever someone pours tea into your tea cup. Finger tapping is not a superstitious gesture, but rather a custom that dates back to the Qing Dynasty (1644-1911). It is a way to silently show appreciation and thanks. Whenever a Chinese friend notices that your tea cup is half empty, he/she will pour tea into your cup to show respect. In turn, you should show your appreciation by tapping your two fingers, normally the index and middle finger, behind your tea cup. Very few Americans understand this common, simple gesture of appreciation.

Another way to show your appreciation is to hold your two hands in front of your chest, with one hand in a fist and the other hand covering the fist. This is a simple way to say "thank you."

These two gestures are a sure way to impress your Chinese friends and a simple way to show your appreciation.

Tip #38 You will be admired for knowing the Chinese culture when you tap with two fingers after someone pours tea into your cup.

Did you know? It takes about 1,000 tiny tea leaves to make one pound of finished tea.

TAPPING WITH TWO FINGERS

Did you know? Iced tea was claimed to be invented at the St. Louis World's Fair in 1904. The weather was hot and no one was drinking hot tea. An enterprising English merchant poured ice into the tea and iced tea became an instant hit.

Being *Even More* Polite

If you want to be even more polite, you can use the two-handed technique anytime you receive or give something, such as business cards, charge cards, gifts, tea cups, etc. As a foreigner, showing respect and understanding of the Chinese culture will greatly enhance your relationship with your Chinese business clients or customers.

<u>Tip #39 Your Chinese friends will feel that you are a true Chinese for being so polite by using two hands to give and to receive.</u>

Did you know? The Chinese government was so embarrassed with how some of their citizens behaved while traveling abroad on holidays that it passed a law making it legally binding for Chinese to respect local customs and traditions even while traveling.

GIVING AND RECEIVING WITH TWO HANDS ARE POLITE GESTURES

Did you know? Chinese believe that courtesy demands mutuality. When someone receives a gift or favor, it is expected to be reciprocated in the future. Reciprocity is necessary to build friendship between the two parties.

Chapter 4

Chinese Dining

Chinese love to eat, and they take their food seriously. The history of Chinese cooking dates back thousands of years. Food and cooking is influenced by location, tradition, and climate. Each region has its unique style, taste, and preparation technique. The Chinese food you see in the United States is most likely Cantonese style, as the majority of the Chinese in the America are from the Canton region. Sichuan cuisine is known for being hot and spicy. Other popular types of regional dishes come from Fujian, Hunan, Shandong and Jiangsu. The most common starches include rice, noodles, and steamed buns.

When it comes to dining, there is great emphasis on respecting customs, culture, and traditions. As a host, or even as a guest, proper etiquette is expected. Good Chinese table manners are thought to bring luck and happiness. Breaking the traditions can bring shame to yourself and your family. As an American, it is important for us to understand and to respect the Chinese dining customs.

Tip #40 Don't eat any street food in China, you will more than likely need to run to the nearest toilet.

Tip #41 In the United States, if you can't find a restaurant to eat on Christmas or New Year, look for a Chinese restaurant.

Did you know? Authentic Chinese food is probably one of the healthiest foods in the world.

LAST BIRTHDAY WISH

Did you know? According to a traditional Chinese doctor, snake powder helps arthritis, eliminates toxins, clears your skin, and keeps you young.

Good Dining Habits

In China, invited guests are treated with high respect and dignity. There are many rules of formality for simple actions such as greeting, seating and eating. These rules should be followed to avoid insult to other guests and the host. Some of the Chinese dining norms may be unfamiliar to Americans. Below, I have listed some helpful tips.

1. Do not sit until the host directs you to do so.
2. Leave the ordering to the host.
3. Even if you are hungry, wait for the host to start eating before you do.
4. Accept everything the host offers you.
5. Never eat the last item on the plate.
6. Let the host make the first toast.
7. If a whole steamed fish is ordered, do not flip the fish over.
8. Know your chopstick etiquette (more on this later).
9. Do not ask for a fortune cookie. Fortune cookies were invented in the United States.

Tip #42 Chinese usually honor you with the best part of the food. If you are afraid to eat it, hide it with other food. Plates are changed quite frequently in better Chinese restaurants.

Tip #43 The tastiest part of the fish is the fish head. It is usually reserved for the honored guest.

Tip #44 Learn how to correctly use chopsticks.

Did you know? The bat is traditional good luck symbol. It is depicted in designs in clothing, crafts, and porcelain – and it is edible.

LAWYERS DO NOT NEED CHOPSTICKS

Chinese proverb: "A lawyer sleeps by lying on one side and then lying on the other side."

Expect the Unexpected When You Invite Someone to Dinner

During a recent trip to Humen, China, I was invited to dinner by my franchisee, Mr. Chen. On the way to dinner, I counted that there were ten of us total. We arrived at an elegant French restaurant. Before entering, we were greeted by Mr. Chen's friend, Mr. Lee. As we entered the restaurant, we were escorted to a large table. To my surprise, there were already people seated. Mr. Lee introduced us to one of the individuals, Mr. Chang, our host for the dinner. It was at this point that I realized the person who invited us, Mr. Chen, did not know the host. We were the uninvited guests.

To my surprise, the host did not complain and in fact welcomed us graciously. He ordered expensive wine and kept toasting all night long. The host was at ease spending a large sum of money to show off his wealth.

When I arrived in Hong Kong two days later, I joked with my cousin, Henry Parwani, about the dinner. Henry told me that he had the same experience in Shanghai. He invited a business associate for dinner. When his business associate arrived, he brought along with him five uninvited friends. Henry said that this custom is becoming common in China.

Tip #44 Always confirm the number of guests who are coming to dine with you.

Tip #45 If you don't like to eat a dish (like the bat), rotate it away before the host can put it on your plate.

Did you know? If you eat at a Chinese buffet in the United States, on average, three full plates will total 3,000 calories.

THE UNINVITED GUESTS

Did you know? Chop Suey is a Chinese dish that originated in the United States. It may have been invented in the 19th century when Chinese laborers were working on the U.S. Transcontinental Railroad. So don't ask for it in a restaurant in China.

The "Lazy Susan"

The Lazy Susan is a round rotating tray or disc in the center of the dining table. It is circular in shape and usually made from wood or glass. The Lazy Susan ensures all the diners have equal access to the dishes.

During the meal, do not rotate the Lazy Susan when someone is taking food from the serving platter. Wait until that person is done, then slowly rotate the Lazy Susan to show respect to others. If you like a dish, do not pile it on your plate but rather take a small quantity and wait for your turn again.

Seating

Seating arrangement depends on the social or business occasion. As a guest, it is safest to observe others and wait for the host to seat you. Never seat yourself without direction from the host. The honored guest is usually seated in the middle, facing the door and the host will normally be seated across the honored guest. On several occasions, my host sat next to me so we could discuss business more intimately. The seats to the right of the guest are assigned according to a descending order of the hierarchy. The least senior people are assigned closer to the door.

Tip #46 Never sit down at the dining table until directed to do so by the host.

Chinese proverb: "Man with one chopstick goes hungry."

PROPER CHINESE SEATING ARRANGEMENT

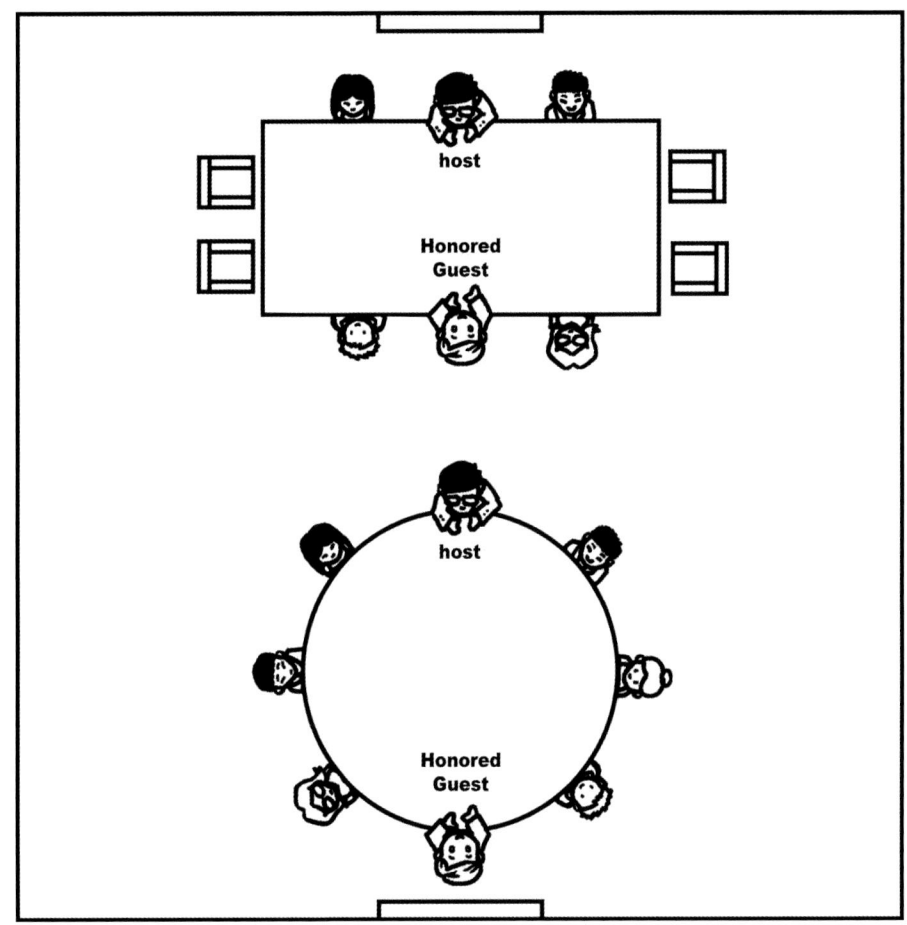

Did you know? President George H. W. Bush's favorite Chinese restaurant, The Peking Gourmet Inn, in Falls Church, Virginia installed a bulletproof window for security.

Private Dining Room

In order to impress your guests, you should pay extra for a private dining room in a Chinese restaurant. The private dining room provides intimacy and amenities over the public dining room. Depending on the restaurant, it can range from a regular room to a fancy dining room. I was invited to a private dining room a couple years ago in Guangzhou by a prospective franchisee who wanted to impress me. The room was almost as large as the restaurant and had only one table in the middle of the room. The amenities included two private washrooms, two televisions, sofas, karaoke, a magnificent view, and four waiters to take care of the six of us.

"Bad" Dining Habits

Be prepared to accept some "bad" Chinese dining habits that are usually unacceptable in the United States.

1. Everyone smoking during dinner.

2. Everyone talking loudly and at once.

3. Talking on cell phones during dinner.

4. Drinking and toasting all throughout dinner.

For the female guests, be aware that there may be a lot of "guy talk." I was having lunch with six male business associates in Nanjing. One of them came from a business meeting and brought along a young female attorney. During dinner, the men were boasting and joking about girlfriends and second wives. At one point, one of the men even asked the young attorney if she was interested in being the girlfriend of his rich friend, and he meant it. The young attorney simply smiled and said no. Everyone burst out laughing.

Tip #47 Make sure you pay extra for a private dining room if you want to impress your clients (Mianzi).

Tip #48 Be ready to drink and get drunk unless you have a good excuse not to drink.

Did you know? There are 300 million smokers in China with over 1.3 million deaths annually from smoking related illness.

CHINESE DINERS WITH CELL PHONES

Did you know? There are two and a half times more cell phones in China than the population of the United States.

Sanitizing Utensils at a Restaurant

In better restaurants in China, you are given a small plate, cup, bowl, and spoon wrapped in clear plastic. Unwrap the chopsticks and remove the clear plastic wrap from the dishes. There should be a hot tea kettle and large bowl on the table. Wash the cup, bowl, fork, chopsticks, and spoon with hot tea. When you are done, pour the dirty tea into the large bowl. Your dishes and utensils are supposed to be sanitized and germ free. If you are confused as to what to do, observe others at your table first, then follow their actions. In most restaurants in China, you have to pay for the napkins. A small package will be brought to you upon request.

While it is easy to enjoy a good Chinese meal, I do not suggest you go inside the kitchen. My friend asked me to help him pick a fresh fish in the kitchen. A diminutive girl selected a five pound live fish in the tank and placed it on the kitchen floor. The fish was struggling so she stepped on the fish tail and used a mallet to hammer its head until the fish died. I lost my appetite for fish for the entire month.

Tip #49 Always bring your own napkin in case there are none at the restaurant.

Did you know? Rice flour was used to strengthen some of the bricks for the Great Wall of China.

CHINESE EXOTIC ANIMAL FOOD ASSOCIATION UNION DEMONSTRATION

Did you know? The best part of a steamed fish dish is the fish head with the eyes staring at you.

Order More Than You Can Eat

A Chinese host will almost certainly order more food than you can eat. I was invited to a dinner in Xiamen once and the host ordered 20 courses. I must have gained three pounds after dinner. Although the meal was sumptuous and delicious, my host kept apologizing to me that it was not enough. Quite often, the host wants to show his generosity and graciousness to the guest by ordering many dishes. It is another way to "save face." You should accept the host's generosity by repeating "it is too much" or "the meal is great."

In United States, we often ask for a doggy bag after the meal. At my family dinners in Hawaii, we bring home everything, even leftover rice. In China, I seldom see the host take any leftovers home after a business dinner, no matter how much food is left over. He pays the bill and simply walks away. It is another way for him to flaunt his wealth (Mianzi).

Tip #50 Do not ask for a doggy bag in China. You will lose face.

Tip #51 Eat small portions and eat slowly. There will be more dishes to come.

Did you know? Chinese girls are warned about leaving uneaten rice in their bowls which means that there will be scars on their future husband's face.

TOO MUCH FOOD

Did you know: To save face, your Chinese host will order more food than you can eat. Be sure to eat slowly and in small portions.

Chopstick Etiquette

Learning how to use chopsticks is a must in China. Most Chinese will admire you for attempting it. Your desire to even attempt to use chopsticks is a show of respect of Chinese culture and most Chinese will welcome it. Chopsticks are fairly easy to learn. Before you go to China, visit a Chinese restaurant and practice. I have three illustrations to help you learn how to use the chopsticks.

Once you master the use of chopsticks, learn basic chopsticks etiquette.

1. Do not point your chopsticks at anyone.
2. Do not play with your chopsticks.
3. Do not leave your chopsticks sticking vertically in the food.
4. Do not drop your chopsticks. If you do, ask for a new set.
5. Do not dig around the dish for food.
6. Do not wave your chopsticks when you are talking.
7. Do not place your chopsticks on the table. Use the chopsticks holder or your plate.
8. Do not serve other people with your chopsticks. Use the serving utensils.

Tip #52 You have to practice until you master the use of chopsticks.

Tips #53 Never point your chopsticks at someone when you are talking.

Did you know? The Chinese started to utilize chopsticks about 5,000 years ago. 60 to 80 billion disposable chopsticks are used each year, and that is equivalent to 20 million trees.

HOW TO USE CHOPSTICKS

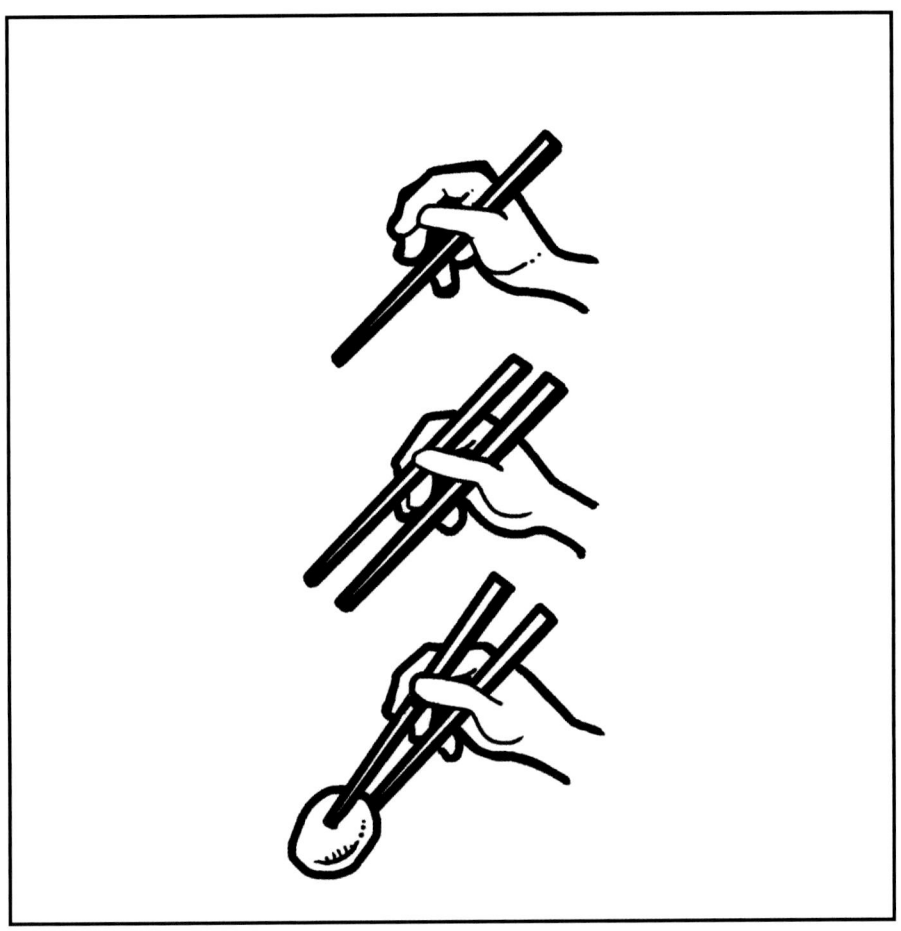

- Step One: One chopstick is held between the thumb and rests on the third finger.
- Step Two: The other chopstick is held between the thumb and the base of the first two fingers.
- Step Three: Practice by bringing the chopsticks together.

Did you know? Eighty percent of the chopsticks that are made in Japan are from a little town called OBAMA.

The Art of Drinking Tea

A Chinese legend claims that tea was discovered in China around 2737 B.C. by an emperor when a tea leaf accidentally fell into his hot cup of water. Tea is the most popular and important drink in China. You will find a set of tea making instruments in every home. Even in most hotels, instead of a coffee maker, you will find a tea kettle.

In most Chinese dining, tea etiquette plays an important role. As soon as you are seated, the host will immediately pour tea into your cup. A simple "thank you" and tapping of your two fingers is a show of appreciation. Invariably, as soon your cup is half empty, your host will immediately fill up your cup immediately. If you do not want any more tea, just leave your cup full. Always offer someone tea before you serve yourself.

Tip #54 The proper way to pour tea is by holding the tea pot with your right hand and using your left hand to hold the tea cover.

Tip #55 When the tea pot is empty, open the tea pot cover half way as a signal for the waiter to refill the tea pot.

Did you know? The most expensive tea in China is Dao Hong Pao, a type of oolong tea. One ounce of Dao Hong Pao tea leaves can cost up to $35,435.

CHOPSTICKS FOR DUMMIES

Chinese proverb: "Better to be deprived of food for three days than tea for one day."

Ask for Rice

In United States, we are accustomed to serving rice with our Chinese meals. In China, however, rice is rarely served unless you ask for it. Since your gracious Chinese host wants to treat you to the best and most expensive dishes, rice may not be part of the menu. If you ask for rice, the host may feel offended.

Tip #56 In China, if you want to eat rice, you have to ask for it.

Noodles for Longevity

Noodle dishes are important to Chinese dining especially for special occasions like birthdays and weddings. I catered a birthday party for a long time customer. I brought extra food but I forgot to bring noodles. My loyal customer did not say anything to me. He simply never returned to my L & L Hawaiian Barbecue restaurant.

Noodles symbolize longevity in Chinese culture. It is also a metaphor for a long life. So cutting noodles with a knife may mean destruction or death. Therefore, slurping noodles is totally acceptable in Chinese dining.

Tip #57 Make sure to order noodles for a Chinese birthday celebration.

Did you know? Marco Polo brought Chinese noodles and ice cream back to Italy – likely the source for spaghetti and gelato!

ESCAPE FROM BEING STIR-FRIED DOBERMEIN

Did you know? Eating dog meat on the summer solstice is a local custom in Yulin, a small city in southern China. The Yulin Summer Solstice Dog Meat Festival is held every year. The Chinese believe that the dog meat will bring healthy days during the winter.

Fighting for the Bill (Mianzi)

In the United States, we are accustomed to splitting a bill after a meal. The Chinese fight for the bill as a show of respect and hospitality. It may look like a fist fight and quite often the bill gets ripped into pieces. It is a great show after a good meal!

If I am a guest, I should never pay for the bill, no matter how poor the host is. It is extremely rude to the host. Even though you are not paying the bill, you still need to fight for it. When fighting for the bill, make sure the host has the opportunity to pay for it. If you fail to fight for the bill, it may imply that the host owes you a favor. You should argue for the bill several times and at the end thank the host for his hospitality. I call this style of fighting for the bill "alligator technique".

As for my Chinese social friends or acquaintances, we still have to fight for the bill. However, a more common method is taking turns to win the bill. This way everyone has a chance to pay.

Tip #58 If you really want to pay for the bill, arrive early at the restaurant and pay in cash before your friends arrive.

If you really do not want to pay for the bill, learn some of the techniques that I observed to avoid paying the dining bill.

Tip #59 When you see the waiter coming with the bill, rush to the restroom.

Tip #60 Fight for the bill with your left (or non-dominant) hand.

Tip #61 Sit away from where the waiter serves the food. That is where the bill will come.

Tip #62 After the meal, place your plate, cup, and bowl in front of you so there is no room for the waiter to place the check.

Tip #63 Tell your friends that you are not feeling well and have to leave early.

Tip # 64 If nothing works; tell your friends that you cannot find your wallet. You will definitely lose face.

Did you know? Asking the host or guest to split a bill in a restaurant is very embarrassing and insulting in China.

ALLIGATORS HAVE NO CHANCE FOR THE BILL

Did you know? You should never let someone else pay the bill without at least fighting for it. Act like an alligator with short hands.

Eating Exotic Food

I was invited to try some exotic cuisine in Zhongshan twenty years ago. I was reluctant, but my host was an old friend I had not seen in many years. Although I was familiar with eating chicken feet, pig's feet, intestine, and pig's blood, nothing prepared me for this meal of rats and worms. I found the dishes very distasteful. I have listed some exotic dishes that you may find in China.

- **Qinghai** – sheep vein, stir-fried camel foot, and yak vein.

- **Hubei** – snake meat and crocodile claws.

- **Sichuan** – duck intestines, pig brain, and rabbit ears.

- **Hunan** – spicy frog legs, tripe, and sea cucumbers.

- Dog, monkey brain, rat, mice, cat, and sea snake are some of the most exotic dishes in China.

Tip #65 When you are in Beijing, visit Wangfujing Snack Street for a real experience of exotic food. You can stay away from the bugs and snake delicacies and stick to your conventional Chinese food.

Tips #66 Just eat without asking and looking at what you are eating.

Did you know? The Chinese find that some Western food as distasteful such as deer testicle, fish eggs, sheep brains, snails, rare steak, and goose liver.

CHINESE EAT EVERYTHING, DEAD OR ALIVE

Chinese proverb: "Anything that walks, swims, crawls, or flies with its back to heaven is edible."

Toothpick Etiquette

Toothpicks are made available to diners after each meal. The proper way to use the toothpick is by covering your mouth while using the toothpick. When you are done, place the toothpick on your bowl or plate. It is rude and inconsiderate to leave the toothpick on the table or throw it on the floor. Finally, do not play with the toothpick.

Tip #67 Cover your mouth when you are using a toothpick.

Did you know: You can sell your old toothpicks in Kulang, China. There are seven recycle centers that will pay 35 cents for each pound of used toothpicks.

THE ORIGIN OF TOOTHPICKS

Did you know? The toothpick has been around for a long time. It existed before the arrival of modern humans.

After Dinner Entertainment

Karaoke is the most popular entertainment activity in China. Karaoke venues range from small and inexpensive to large, multi-level, ornate palaces. The rooms come in different sizes to accommodate your budget and taste. The rooms are equipped with televisions, microphones, sofas, and possibly a washroom. You can order food, drink, and whatever else you might need. The rooms are loud with music and filled with smoke. It is a popular place for business entertaining and special occasions like birthdays, bachelor parties or a night out.

During my visits to China, my friends and business associates would always invite me to an evening at the local karaoke bar after dinner. I hate loud music and smoke-filled rooms. I try not to offend my friends by saying that I am very tired or not feeling well. Well, my friends now call me the sick man from Hawaii.

Tip #68 If you want to impress your friends and business associates, learn to sing a couple of popular Chinese songs. You will be a big hit.

Tip #69 Unless you like to party, it is better to stay back in your hotel. The karaoke room will be filled with cigarette smoke and extremely noisy.

Did you know? A karaoke bar is probably the most popular after dinner entertainment in China. There are over 100,000 karaoke bars in China, which is almost ten times more than the number of movie theaters.

CHOICE OF AMERICAN OR CHINESE FOOD

Did you know? In 1873, twenty five ducks were imported from China to Long Island. Only nine survived. The Peking or Long Island duck became the most popular duck breed for eggs and meat in the United States.

Chapter 5
Doing Business in China

China has become an attractive place to invest. Major global giants such as Starbucks, McDonald's, GM, and Volkswagen have established a foothold in China. However, the country remains difficult to do business in due to intense competition, unfamiliar business etiquette, and the language barrier.

While this book is written specifically with China in mind, most of the customs and traditions may be similar for doing business with Chinese in Hong Kong, Taiwan or other countries. However, keep in mind that there is much dissimilarity within China itself. With over 1.34 billion people, local and provincial customs and traditions are unavoidable.

In Hawaii, a project to build an L & L Hawaiian Barbecue will take about eight to ten months from start to completion. The building permit alone takes at least three months. My franchisee in China told me that the restaurant will be done in 30 days and that all the permits will be ready at the grand opening.

Tip #70 You need Guanxi if you want to do business in China.

Tip #71 Remember that foreign companies seldom make money in China.

Chinese proverb: "To open a shop is easy; to keep it open is an art."

BRAGGING TO THE WRONG PEOPLE

Did you know? The Maglev train in Shanghai is the fastest commercial train in the world. It reaches a speed of 267 miles per hour. The 19 mile trip from the airport to town takes less than eight minutes, with the train achieving a top speed of 267 mph and averaging 165 mph.

Do Your Homework and Be Prepared

China's impressive economic growth has attracted many new businesses, especially since opening up to the foreign market in the 1978. Chinese customs and rules are challenging and perplexing. When you decide to do business in China, you have to develop a comprehensive plan. Look at your company's resources and commitments. The following four steps are critical:

1. Conduct a full market research;
2. Send your management team to China to do further study;
3. Hire consultants from China to assist your company; and
4. Talk to people who have done business in China.

Doing business in China is extremely risky. There are many scams and unscrupulous people. In 2013, Caterpillar wrote off $580 million in losses on an acquisition in China. The company was duped by accounting irregularities and fraud. If you are careless, you will suffer the consequences. There are many horror stories to tell about doing or trying to do business in China.

Tip #72 Learn the lessons from all those who failed in China.

Did you know? China is the world's largest market for automobiles, cellphones, and seafood.

YOU GET WHAT YOU PAY FOR

Chinese proverb: "You pay peanuts, you get a monkey."

Do Not Rush Into Any Deal

Doing business in China takes time and patience. If you rush into a business deal, it will more than likely have poor results. Your Chinese counterpart may not be the right person. You need to do the right research and make certain that the business proposition is feasible and your Chinese partner is trustworthy and dependable. The faster you start a business in China, the sooner you lose your investment. Rushing into a deal is an invitation to failure. You have to plan for success.

Tip #73 Be patient and do all your research before investing in China.

Build a Local Team

Before you begin investing in China, you need to build a solid team that you can trust and depend on. China is thousands of miles from United States, and it is impossible for you to be traveling constantly. Before you know it, you will get burned out. You either need to have someone in your company relocate or find a business partner that you can rely on. You need someone who can understand the culture and complexities of the China market, they must also be able to speak Mandarin, and most importantly, be someone you trust. Make sure you do a complete background check and reference check on all your partners and hires.

Several years ago, L & L Hawaiian Barbecue wanted to print calendars for our restaurants. We researched on Alibaba.com, a Chinese website, for printers. We found a company with a beautiful website and with impressive photos of the printing factory. The prices were very reasonable. I made a surprise visit to the printing company in Zhongshan, and I found that it was just a mail drop. You never know what to expect in China unless you make a trip to visit it.

Tip #74 You must visit China and find a local partner before doing business in the country.

Did you know? Alibaba.com is the largest e-commerce site based in China. It has over 24,000 employees, which is more than Yahoo and Facebook combined.

CHINA IS MORE EXPENSIVE THAN YOU THINK

Did you know? Don't assume a Mr. Wang is married to a Mrs. Wang in Beijing. There are over 1.5 million people with the family name Wang in Beijing.

American Standards and Products May Not Work in China

Do not bring your American approach of doing business to China. There is a great difference in doing things in America and China. This book has shown many examples where Chinese culture and business etiquette is unlike what we are used to in America. We should learn and study the Chinese way of doing business before investing in China. During an interview, Larry Namer, co-founder and president of Metan Development Group, told of an experience he had on a project. He visited the project three days before a photo shoot was scheduled. To his surprise, nothing had been built. Other than Larry, no one was concerned or worried about it. By the day of the shoot, the set was miraculously completed. Things are done differently in China.

I had a similar experience when my franchisee opened the first L & L Hawaiian Barbecue in China. He told me that the restaurant would open thirty days after the lease was signed. I thought he was joking until he called me to attend the grand opening on the 28th day.

Tip #75 You may unknowingly be a partner with the Chinese government, directly or indirectly.

Did you know? The Chinese government controls most of China's financial sectors and much of the country's productive assets through direct and indirect ownership.

NO QUESTIONS ASKED RETURN POLICY

Did you know? In China, a watermelon is one of the most popular gifts to bring to a host. China is also the top producer of watermelons in the world.

Adapt to the Local Market

China has over 1.34 billion people. The country is so diverse that there is no true consumer profile. What works in Beijing, may not work in Shanghai. Foreign businesses have to adapt and adjust to the market. You need to talk to trade organizations, the local chamber of commerce, potential customers, and the competition to understand the market. There is no simple solution in the Chinese market. You simply have to adjust to the taste of the Chinese consumers to find the right combination for success.

When McDonald's opened in China, it had to try many times to find the right combination of menu items. If you order breakfast at McDonald's, you will find congee (rice porridge), noodles, and rice. Starbucks serves green tea lattes, which is actually preferred over the vanilla latte by the Chinese consumers. Even at L & L Hawaiian Barbecue, we added many local dishes. We plan to continue making changes until we find the right combination.

Tip #76 When you are in China, sell what the Chinese want.

Did you know? KFC has more locations than McDonald's in China. Currently, there are over 4,600 locations in 950 cities.

AMERICAN FAST FOOD ADJUSTS TO CHINESE TASTE

Did you know? McDonald's sells squid ink burger and rice bowls. KFC offers congee (rice porridge) and lotus root. Dunkin' Donuts has pork and seaweed donuts.

Expect to Be Copied

I learned the hard way that Chinese entrepreneurs will copy your concept or idea before you can blink. When I started L & L Hawaiian Barbecue in California and trademarked Hawaiian Barbecue, it was a new fast food concept of Asian American dining. It was very successful. In less than two months, there was an imitation L & L operated by a former Chinese restaurant cook.

In China, you can expect the same type of copycat but even faster. KFC was very successful but there must be at least 10 brands that are pretty similar. There are computer stores that look like Apple, but are imitations. The Chinese government tried to close down all the manufacturers of fake European designer bags. The ingenious Chinese entrepreneurs started to make the fake bags in moving trucks. It is impossible to stop a copycat. You need to devise a plan and compete on the strength of service and brand.

Aggressiveness is part of the Chinese nature. I was waiting in a long line at a market in Xi'an last year. There was an old and frail looking lady behind me. I paused for a second to look at an item to my right. Before I knew it, the old lady was in front of me. The Chinese are aggressive and will copy your concept very fast.

Tip #77 When you register a trademark, make sure you register your trademark's Chinese name, too.

Did you know? Fake chicken eggs were sold as real chicken eggs in China. The fake eggs taste almost like the real egg and cost much less to produce.

WATCH FOR COPYCATS

Did you know? In Kunming, China, there was a counterfeit Apple Store with identical logos and uniforms. Even the employees thought the Apple Store was a genuine one.

Face to Face Meetings

Chinese love having face to face meetings prior to closing any business deals. Chinese build their relationship through frequent face to face relationships. They enjoy an amicable atmosphere to facilitate and build a more personal relationship through gift giving, dining, entertaining, and compliments. You get better results when you meet with your Chinese counterpart face to face.

It also helps to know what your Chinese counterpart is doing. My franchisee asked me for photo of President Obama visiting Hawaii. When I arrived at the L & L Hawaiian Barbecue in Humen, I saw that my franchisee had made a gigantic billboard of President Obama digitally manipulated to be standing in front of an L & L Hawaiian Barbecue.

Tip #78 Face to face meeting is a necessity in China.

Did you know? When a Chinese person asks if you have eaten, it does not mean that he is inviting you to eat. Rather, it is a form of greeting.

TOUGH CHINESE COMPETITION

Did you know? You can get the death penalty in China not only for murder, but also for nonviolent crimes such as drug trafficking and fraud.

Join the Lions Club

The Lions Club in China has the same status as our prestigious private clubs in the United States. Most of the members of the Lions Club in China are business owners and wealthy individuals. Many of the members are women. They do a lot of volunteer work and meet regularly for business networking.

I traveled with one of my staff members, Andrew Lee, to Shenzhen several years ago. Andrew was a former president of the Chinatown Lions Club in Honolulu. During a luncheon meeting, I noticed that one of the ladies at the table was wearing a Lions Club pin. I casually mentioned that Andrew was the former president of the Lions Club in Honolulu. She was so excited, and she called the Lions Club in Guangzhou. In less than one hour, she arranged for the Lions Club in Guangzhou to host a dinner to honor Andrew. When we arrived, there were thirty members waiting for us in the Lions Club's fancy restaurant. Andrew was the guest of honor and the VIP. You will never find this type of fanfare and reception in the United States. Lions Club in China is much respected and also a great place to network for business.

Tip #79 Join the local Lions Club in the United States before you go to China for business.

Tip #80 If you wear your Lions Club pin on your jacket, you will receive special recognition and attention.

Did you know? The Lions Club was first established in Guangdong and Shenzhen in 2001 and was the first service club recognized by the Chinese government.

CHINESE FOOD TAKE-OUT

Did you know? There are more than 100 cities in China that have more than one million in population. There are only ten cities in the United States of that size. The fast food market in China is unlimited.

Prepare to Bargain

The Chinese love to bargain and to haggle. They believe that there is always room for negotiation on every deal. You can expect multiple negotiation sessions before a deal is consummated. Even after you have agreed and signed a binding contract, they will continue to haggle with you. It is so frustrating, but this is what I have learned to expect after dealing with the Chinese over the past 60 years. The Chinese will haggle you to death.

<u>Tip #81 Start at a high number and expect a long negotiation.</u>

Did you know? Bargaining is part of the Chinese heritage. They will haggle even over a penny.

WILL YOU ACCEPT MY FINAL OFFER?

Did you know? Your biggest leverage in bargaining is time. You can always walk away and return later.

Gift Giving

Gifts may be given as a token of appreciation and gratitude. Knowing the Chinese culture and customs can help you avoid unintentional embarrassment and insult. During a delegation visit, the gift should be given to the head of the Chinese organization at the end of an introductory meeting. The gift should be inexpensive and preferably from your home state. I usually bring a small Hawaii-made memento such as a box of Hawaiian macadamia nut chocolates. Make sure you avoid giving knives, clocks, books, and especially anything that is black or white, which may suggests bad luck or death. You should present the gift with both hands and receive it likewise.

President George Bush committed a big blunder in 1989 by giving Chinese Premier Li Peng a pair of black Texas cowboy boots. The soles of the feet are considered the lowest and dirtiest part of the body. It was a prodigious insult to the Chinese premier.

Tip #82 Check with your local Chinese friends before buying a gift for a friend in China.

Did you know? Buddha once said, "If you know what I know about the power of giving, you would not let a single meal pass without sharing with someone."

EVERYTHING IS MADE IN CHINA

Did you know? Seventy percent of the world's umbrellas, eighty-five percent of all America's Christmas lights, sixty percent of the world's buttons, and seventy-two percent of America's shoes are made in China.

Dress Properly

Times have changed and Western clothes are pretty normal in modern China. During business meetings, make sure you dress appropriately. It is a sign of respect and sincerity.

- **Men**: A dark suit and tie for important business meetings and banquets. Even for causal meetings, I wear a jacket with at least a polo shirt.
- **Women**: Dress conservatively without revealing necklines and without flashy jewelry. Stay away from skimpy or revealing clothing.

Last year I visited my L & L location in Humen. During the meeting with my franchisee, I dressed in business attire. After a long meeting, I went back to my hotel. In the afternoon, I decided to make a quick visit to the restaurant, which was located across the street from my hotel. Being from Hawaii, I wore shorts, t-shirts and slippers (flip-flops). When I arrived at the restaurant, I noticed that the employees were staring at me. My franchisee came out and commented that I was super casual. I realized that my clothing was inappropriate. I was dressed below my social status as the president of the company.

China is known for making fake European designer products. They are sold to tourists and those who cannot afford the authentic product. Most of the well-heeled Chinese, however, only purchase the genuine designer products. It is a status symbol. If you are caught wearing counterfeit designer product, it could imply that you are not in the same class status and you could lose face.

Tip #83 Do not wear bright red colors, which are for celebration or white clothes and shoes, which are for funerals and connote death.

Tip #84 China has a high luxury tax. It is cheaper to buy European designer products in the United States.

Did you know? In ancient China, the Chinese carried tiny dog breeds in their sleeves to stay warm during the winter.

CHINESE LEARN TO SPEAK ITALIAN INSTANTLY

Did you know? Although there are more Gucci and Chanel stores in China than in the United States, the Chinese prefer to buy overseas because they are afraid of buying a counterfeit in China.

Compete by Pricing

The Chinese have a compulsion to compete by pricing. They think that lowering prices will drive more business. A Chinese buffet came to Los Angeles many years ago. The cost was about $12.95 per person. Shortly after, there was a proliferation of Chinese buffet restaurants. Today, you can eat in a Chinese buffet restaurant for $5.95.

Do not try to compete against the Chinese by lowering prices. Rather, work on the service and quality of the product. I found that a foreign brand commands a premium to the price.

<u>Tip #85 An American brand in China brings in a higher value. The Chinese trust Americans quality and workmanship.</u>

Did you know? China has lower rent, salaries, benefits, taxes, and transportation costs for operating a business. You cannot compete against the Chinese based on price.

CHINESE COMPETITION IS CUT THROAT

Chinese proverb: "Cheap things are not good, good things are not cheap."

Prepare for Failure

I have heard more failure stories than success stories about Americans doing business in China over the past 30 years. Most business ventures do not work out in China. I remember when China was first opened for foreign investments. Many companies from Hawaii were the first to tackle the China market. Very few succeeded. Lessons were learned and past mistakes were corrected. But it is still very difficult to have a profitable business venture in China. There are too many variables, such as customs, government regulations, and the language barrier. Be ready for an exit strategy.

Tip #86 Plan your exit strategy before you enter into the Chinese market.

Did you know? There are many unsuccessful and struggling American businesses in China such as eBay, Best Buy, Google, Mattel, and Taco Bell.

A REQUIEM FOR FAILURE

Did you know? In China, competition in business comes quickly. Before you can blink your eyes, your competition will be there.

Chapter 6
Travel

To truly understand the history, culture, business, and people of China, it is important for you to visit this incredible country. During the past 30 years, I have traveled to China two to three times annually. Yet, I am still amazed at the rapid development of the country. The landscape is so vast and diverse. There are big sprawling cities, small ancient villages, rivers, mountains, deserts, and plains. China is modern and ancient, oftentimes both at once. China has modern transportation like the Maglev train in Shanghai but also mule driven carts in Ying Mi Gorge.

Let's look at the four reasons for you to visit China.

1. **Sights**: There are so many ancient sights you can visit. The Great Wall and the Terracotta Warriors are a once in a lifetime experience. Beautiful landscapes in Guilin or Zhangjiajie (where the movie, Avatar was filmed) are some of the best sights I have visited in the world.

2. **Food**: The food in China is simply the best. You should leave your experience of your Chinese food behind in America. Every village, city, region, and province has its own specialty and taste. There are so many different cuisines that you will not know where to start.

3. **Shopping**: China is known as a shopper's paradise. You can buy almost anything at bargain prices. Most visitors purchase an extra suitcase to return home.

4. **History**: China is modernizing rapidly. Many ancient villages, heritage sites, and landscapes may disappear sooner than you think. If you do not visit China soon, some of the heritage sites may be gone forever.

Tip #87 Your first trip in China should include these four cities, Beijing, Shanghai, Xi'an, and Hong Kong (take a day trip to Macau).

Tip #88 Don't be afraid to try any food. Just don't ask what it is.

Tip #89 You have to bargain for everything.

Tip # 90 See China now before the heritage sites start to disappear.

Chinese proverb: "Walking ten thousand miles of the world is better than reading ten thousand books."

LOST IN TRANSLATION

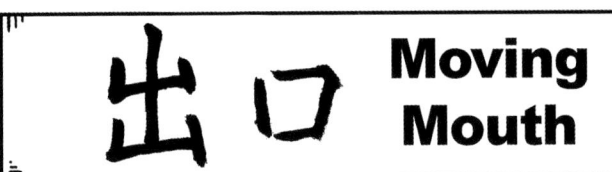

(EXIT)

(RUBBISH CONTAINER)

I Like Your Smile but You Look Like You Put Your Shoes on My Face

(DO NOT STEP ON GRASS)

Did you know? During the Bejing Olympics in 2008, the Chinese government made massive efforts to eliminate Chinglish on signs and menus in Beijing.

Where to Find the Best Travel Deals to China

If you want the best travel deals to China, you should consider contacting the Chinese travel agencies in your local Chinatown. Most of these travel agencies have extensive connections, arrangements, and contacts in China. I always compare prices with the top online travel brokers, and most of the time, the Chinese travel agencies have the lower price. These travel agencies specialize in the China market and many act as consolidators for airlines and hotels. They deal with the China travel agencies on a daily basis and are better equipped to help you with your travel to China.

Most of these Chinatown agencies offer a one stop service for China. They can book your airfare, hotel, land arrangement, and even apply a China visa, for a fee. I frequently use Skyway Express Travel in Honolulu for my China visa. Peggy Luu even takes my passport photo as part of the application. Whenever I need land or hotel arrangement, Henry Ou, the owner of Air & Sea Travel Center in Honolulu, takes care of me and gives me the best deal.

I was pleasantly surprised to find senior discounts to museums, shows, transportation and to various activities in China. However, it is not available all the time, you have to ask.

Tip #91 Find your best China deal with travel agencies in your local Chinatown.

Tip #92 Always ask for senior discounts for admission and transportation.

Lao Tzu once said, "A journey of a thousand miles must begin with a single step."

ALWAYS ASK FOR SENIOR DISCOUNT

Did you know? China has the largest senior population in the world. The number of individuals older than 60 is approximately 128 million.

Money Exchange

China's currency is called the Yuan or RMB (ren-min-bi). Before you leave for China, you should exchange a small amount for taxis and incidentals. Keep in mind the exchange rate is probably much better in China at the local hotels or banks. The exchange rates are pretty standard. In most of the hotels, they may set a limit for the amount you are cashing. Banks are better places to exchange, but you will need to bring your passport. However, be aware, most bank officers probably cannot speak English.

Tip #93 Bring crisp U.S. currency. Do not carry old, wrinkled or marked U. S. currency.

Did you know? The Ming Dynasty issued paper money around 1375. The largest currency in China is 100 RMB. It is approximately 16 U.S. dollars.

NO COMPLAINTS FOR WORKING OVERTIME

Did you know? Most Chinese workers welcome overtime to earn extra money. It is not unusual for them to work 60 hours a week without complaints.

Hotels in China

China is experiencing tremendous growth in hotel construction, especially luxury brands such as Ritz-Carlton and Inter-Continental. The growth has even proliferated lower profile cities such as Hualue in Chengdu and Qufu in the Shandong province. The Chinese government is wholeheartedly supporting international tourists visiting China.

The hotel industry has gone through a lot of changes since China opened up to global travel. Most of the Western brands offer better amenities and comfort to attract domestic and international tourists. Generally speaking, the hotel room rate is lower in China than the United States. In larger cities, however, such as Beijing and Shanghai, the rates are comparable to New York City or San Francisco.

When you stay at a hotel in China, do not judge the service or amenities by the American industry standard. In smaller cities, the front desk may not be able to speak English or the receptionist may sound rude. This is especially true for the local Chinese brand hotels that cater to domestic travel.

In most hotels in China, I found that the bed is lower to the ground and the mattress is stiff. This is quite common even in Western brand hotels. I found a solution by requesting extra thick blankets and laying them on top of the mattress. The blankets heighten the bed and add cushion.

I love to watch news channels such as CNN and BBC. In China, unless you stay in a Western brand hotel, you probably will not get any English speaking television channels. It is very frustrating to not have any English speaking television programs, especially when I am visiting for a long period of time. Fortunately, while staying in Liangshan, I accidentally found the China Central Television English News station (CCTV) which occasionally runs some English programs.

Tip #94 Most Americans use Expedia, Orbitz, Hotel.com to look for hotel rooms in China. For even lower rate, check Ctrip.com, a Chinese website for local hotels.

Tip #95 You should pay or upgrade to Club Room level. The food and facilities are first class in China. It is worth the extra money.

Did you know? The number of overseas tourists visiting China exceeded 55 million in 2010. China is the third most visited country in the World behind France and the United States.

A NOSTALGIC 5-STAR CHINESE HOTEL BIDET

Did you know? The top five rated hotels in China by Conde' Nast Traveler are: (1) Ritz-Carlton Shanghai, Pudong, (2) St. Regis Lhasa Resort, (3) Puli Hotel and Spa, Shanghai, (4) Pudong Shangri-la, Shanghai, and (5) Waldorf Astoria Hotel, Shanghai.

Shop Like a Local and Eat Like a Local

The days of "bargain basement" vacations in China are gone. Let's look at the three major expenses for your travel - shopping, food and lodging. You will find in some areas the cost is even higher than in the United States.

Depending where you shop and what you buy, the shopping could be more or less costly. Local products are still a bargain but foreign made items are much more expensive than what you would pay in New York or London. If you visit Beverly Hills, you will see Chinese tourists standing in line to buy European designer products such as Gucci and Armani or Swiss made watches like Rolex. The Chinese tourists have one of the highest spending averages at over $400 each day. They shop in the United States because it is less expensive than in China for Western brand products. It really depends on what you are planning to buy. China made products such as clothing, electronics, and local products are the best bets.

Dining is not always cheap in China. Recently, I ate with four friends at a dim sum restaurant in Guangzhou. The bill was more than what I pay in Honolulu. You can have a lobster dish in Monterey Park, Los Angeles for probably half the price in Shanghai. You have to eat where the locals eat for a good deal.

As for the hotels, foreign brands such as Sheraton, Sofitel or Pullman could add 20% to 40% to your bill. There are many five stars Chinese brand hotels that are comparable to United States standard. However, most of the receptionists in most of the Chinese brand hotel are unable to speak English.

Tip #96 If you want to save money in China, eat like a local, live like a local, and buy like a local.

Did you know? Hong Kong, Shanghai, and Beijing are three of the top ten most expensive cities in Asia.

THE CRANE IS THE NEW BIRD IN CHINA

Did you know? China is in the midst of a construction boom. Seventy-five percent of the world's tallest construction cranes are in China.

Internet

Internet is very accessible in China. The number of users in China is more than double the number in the United States. The Chinese government has tight control of the internet service as it perceives the internet as a political threat to the country. You can expect censorship from some of your favorite websites, including news and social media accounts.

Most hotels offer free internet and wi-fi service. Some hotels may charge a nominal fee of 30 RMB to 100 RMB. Make sure you bring your mobile phone, iPad, or laptop with wireless service for connection. Internet cafes are available in most cities and are very easy to access. The fee ranges from 5 RMB to 30 RMB for each hour.

Tip #97 Bring your mobile phone, tablet, or laptop with wi-fi connection.

Did you know? There are 591 million internet users in China. Eighty percent of the users are between ten to forty years old.

THIS DOG CAN READ ANYTHING ON THE INTERNET

Did you know? China is the first country to label internet addiction as a clinical disorder. It has many internet addiction camps to treat the addiction.

To Tip or Not to Tip

China is a great place to visit because you don't have to worry about tipping. Tipping is not part of the Chinese culture. Some Chinese may even consider tipping as an insult. During my early visits in China, I would leave a small tip for the housekeepers. When I settled my hotel bill with the front desk, I was told that I left something behind by mistake. Taxi drivers and waiters do not expect a tip. However, in Western hotels that cater to foreigners, tipping the bellman and concierge is acceptable. This is mostly influenced by Western tourists who stay at the hotels.

Another exception will be tour guides that cater to foreign tourists. Most of them rely on tips as part of their income since their pay is so low.

<u>Tip #98 You do not have to tip in China except in some Western hotels.</u>

Did you know? China is on pace to surpass the United States as the world's most dominant business travel market by 2016.

TOO CHEAP TO TIP BUT FACE THE CONSEQUENCE

Did you know? China is a country where tipping is rare. Tipping accentuates a class difference between the rich and the poor. It may result in losing face and respect to the person receiving the tip.

Safety in China

China is a very safe place to travel. Crime rate is relatively low in comparison with major American cities. I had a meeting with the police chief in Guangzhou several years ago. We were discussing the murder rates in Los Angeles and Chicago. He was shocked to know the number of people that were murdered in just one weekend in Chicago. His comment was "we don't even have that many people killed in one year." Violent crime is very rare in China, but you can expect petty crimes like pickpocketing and some purse snatching. Whenever you are in crowded place, make sure you hang tight to your valuables.

The biggest danger, in my opinion, is the safety of the pedestrians due to reckless drivers. Other than the major cities, walking, even on the sidewalk can be dangerous. You may have motorcycles or bicycles going in both directions at full speed. Crossing the street could be a death trap as vehicles do not always stop for the pedestrians. Whenever you have to cross the street, you are risking your life. You do not know where the cars, bicycles, or motorcycles are turning or coming from.

Tip # 99 If you must cross the street, walk slowly at the same pace. You have to keep looking left and right to avoid being run over.

Did you know? China has three percent of the world's vehicles but it has twenty four percent of the fatalities. The death rate for auto accidents in China is more than five times the United States.

WHAT DOES THE TRAFFIC SIGN MEAN?

Did you know? The record for the worst traffic jam in the world was in August 2010 in Beijing. Cars and trucks were trapped in a 62 mile log jam for 12 days.

Do Not Travel on Major Chinese Holidays

Traveling in China during the major holidays can be a nightmare. Right before and right after the Chinese lunar year are the busiest times of the year for travel. Last year, it took me almost four hours to cross the border from Shenzhen to Hong Kong. The long queue was a terrible experience that I will never forget. The three major Chinese holidays are the Chinese lunar year which is between January 21st and February 19th, International Worker's Day on May 1st, and China's national day (equivalent to our Fourth of July) on October 1st.

Tip #100 To enjoy a pleasant Chinese vacation, stay away from the three major holidays.

Did you know? Chinese parents usually nag their daughters for being single during the Lunar New Year. To solve the problem, China has an online service for fake boyfriend rental. The package comes with a free embrace and hand holding.

AFRICAN MIGRATION VS. CHINESE LUNAR YEAR MIGRATION

Did you know? In China, the number of people traveling during the 15-day period of Chinese Lunar Year exceeds 2 billion people.

Bargain for the Best Deals

China is a bargain hunter's dream for arts and crafts, glassware, embroidery, pottery, replicas, clothing, and anything you can think of. Be prepared to bargain and haggle for everything in China, especially with the street vendors. Even at large department stores, don't be afraid to ask for discounts.

Bargaining requires the creation of a relationship with the merchant. You can start by smiling and showing interest in the product. Oftentimes bargaining will end with yelling and shouting before a final price is settled. Do it for fun, but try not to stress yourself out. Finally, once you buy it, don't expect to be able to return it. Make sure you are happy with it.

I have listed four steps which will improve your bargaining skill.

1. Show interest in the item and mentally set the price you want to pay for it.

2. Make an offer of 10% to 30% of the asking price depending on the value of the item. The higher the price, the lower the offer. Don't be afraid to offend the merchant.

3. Wait for the counter offer and slowly increase your offer until you get what you want to pay.

4. Walk away if you do not get your price and start over again with another merchant. I walked away from a merchant in Xi'an several years ago. The merchant followed me for three blocks harassing me to buy. I could not get rid of him until I decided to walk into a large department store. The merchant was afraid to follow me because he was afraid to enter into a private facility.

Tip #101 To avoid hawkers and hagglers, do not make eye contact, say nothing and walk straight ahead. If that does not work, walk into a department store, hotel or restaurant and stay there until the hawker is gone.

Tip #102 Don't feel bad to walk away from a deal. There will always be another bargain.

Did you know? The top five souvenirs in China are silk, tea, porcelain, handicrafts, and jade.

FAKE CHINESE ANTIQUE

Did you know? More than fifty percent of the counterfeit goods in the world come from China. CDs and DVDs rank as the top counterfeits.

Taxi

The taxi in China is an inexpensive and convenient way to get around and visit the cities. Normally, the taxis will be clean and reliable. The cost is much lower than most other international cities I have visited. Unfortunately, most of drivers do not speak English. You have to be prepared with the proper instructions in Chinese to get to your destination.

When you arrive at the airport, make sure you stand in line for the metered taxi. There will be unlicensed vehicles offering you service at lower prices – I recommend you avoid these. Show your hotel name and destination in English and Chinese. Make sure you have the hotel name in Chinese or a local telephone number of the hotel so he can call and get the directions if needed. I arrived in Shanghai last year and I spoke in broken Mandarin instructing my driver to take me to the Park Hyatt. The driver did not understand my pronunciation of Park Hyatt in Mandarin. Finally, I showed him the local telephone number. He got the proper directions from the hotel staff.

Whenever you need to go somewhere, have the concierge write down the address in Chinese so you can show it to the taxi driver. Make sure to get a business card from the hotel. That way you can point to the card and show it to the taxi driver when you return.

If you are lost and need help, you may have difficulty finding someone who can speak English. Your best bet is look for younger people to help, as they may have taken some English classes in school. I met a Chinese client in Shanghai two months ago. To my surprise, his ten year old daughter spoke impeccable English.

Tip #103 Make sure all instructions are in English and Chinese.

Tip #104 If you get lost, look for younger people who can speak some English.

Did you know? In many cities in China, you can hire a motorcycle, scooter, bicycle, horse carriage and even men carrying you to a scenic mountain as transportation.

EASY TO BUY FAKE GUCCI IN NEW YORK CITY

Did you know? Canal Street in New York City is a mecca for fake designers' handbags, belts, clothing, and watches.

Personal Sanitation

China has done a great job in improving its sanitation facilities since it opened to the West. At the Guangzhou Airport recently, I was amazed at the cleanliness of the entire facility. Labor is cheap and the Chinese government can afford to hire full time attendants to clean the toilets 24 hours daily. In rural areas and older buildings, you will find the sanitation facilities much less desirable. Three years ago, I was visiting the Potala Palace in Tibet and found the toilets to be the worst I have ever experienced. My wife revisited the Potala Palace recently and told me that it has installed brand new toilets.

Personal sanitation is still important when traveling in China. You will be meeting many people and visiting places. Make sure you bring your own alcohol based wipes, tissue papers, and bottled water.

Tip #105 Potala Palace in Tibet is an incredible place to visit.

Did you know? Toilet paper was invented in China around 1300 for the Chinese emperor.

INSTRUCTIONS FOR USING TOILETS

Did you know? The average person spends three years of their life sitting on the toilet. There is a Chinese proverb that says "man who stands on toilet is high on pot".

Making Telephone Calls

Using your cell phone to call from China can be very expensive. Whenever I visit China, I carry my American cell phone and another cell phone that I purchased in China. I have my own Chinese telephone number for my Chinese friends and associates. The Chinese cell phone and calling card are relatively inexpensive. The reception is usually crisp and clear since the Chinese government controls where the antennas are installed.

One lesson that I learned about doing business in China is the importance of a status symbol. I carried a Blackberry for many years. My Chinese friends used to joke about the Blackberry being an antique. One day, I noticed that my friend's ten year old daughter was talking with her own iPhone. When I returned to the United States, I bought my first iPhone. The iPhone is really a status symbol in China.

During one of my dinners in China, I noticed that everyone was on their cell phones constantly. If you want to talk to someone during dinner, you probably have to call that person on his/her cell phone.

Tip #106 Remember your Guanzi (conncction).

Tip #107 Remember your Mianxi (face).

Tip #108 Stop reading this book for free and buy it for your own reference.

Did you know? China has one billion cell phones. It is ranked as the number one country for cell phone usage in the world.

THANK YOU AMERICA FOR EVERYTHING

Did you know? The author listed 108 tips and priced the book at $9.88 because 8 is a lucky number for the Chinese.

How to Order Books

If you want to order additional books for family and friends, please contact us at info@hawaiianbarbecue.com. Higher volume pricing is available.

L & L Franchise, Inc.
931 University Avenue, Suite 202
Honolulu, Hawaii 96826
Phone: 808-951-9888
Fax: 808-951-0888
Email: info@hawaiianbarbecue.com
Website: www.hawaiianbarbecue.com
Facebook: www.facebook.com/hawaiianbarbecue
Twitter: www.twitter.com/hawaiianbarbecue
YouTube: www.youtube.com/hawaiianbarbecue

About the Illustrator

Jon J. Murakami is a freelance cartoonist born and raised in Hawaii. He is best known for his line of "Local Kine" greeting cards, which depict humorous occasions & holidays in Hawaii. His regular comic strips include "Calabash" with the Honolulu Star-Advertiser and "Generation Gap" with the Hawaii Herald. Additionally Jon illustrated several Hawaiian children's picture and board books and self-publishes comic books entitled "Gordon Rider" and "The Ara-Rangers."

About the Authors

Eddie Flores, Jr. was born in Hong Kong to a Filipino father and a Chinese mother. He immigrated to United States with his family when he was 16. Eddie graduated from the University of Hawaii with a bachelor's degree and also earned a master's degree from the University of Oklahoma. Two years after he graduated, Eddie started a real estate company. He bought L & L Drive-Inn as a gift for his mother in 1976. Eddie took over the operation in 1990, and along with his partner, Johnson Kam, they expanded the L & L Hawaiian Barbecue chain into 200 locations worldwide.

Eddie speaks and reads Chinese and has had extensive dealings with Chinese in the United States and in China. He started as a business broker and sold many businesses to Chinese clients. Most of L & L Hawaiian Barbecue franchisees are Chinese. The first L & L Hawaiian Barbecue opened in China in 2012.

Elisia Flores is the proud daughter of Eddie and Elaine Flores. She was born and raised in Honolulu, Hawaii. Elisia holds a bachelor's degree in business administration from the University of Southern California as well as a master's in business administration from the University of California, Los Angeles. Prior to working at L&L Hawaiian Barbecue, Elisia worked at General Electric, traveling domestically and internationally. She has traveled to China on multiple occasions to study and to experience the Chinese culture, history and business environment.